Little Feet, Big Heart

LITTLE FEET, BIG HEART

ONE HOUR THAT CHANGED MY LIFE

NADIA GORDYNSKY

XULON ELITE

Xulon Press Elite
555 Winderley Pl, Suite 225
Maitland, FL 32751
407.339.4217
www.xulonpress.com

Exulon ELITE

© 2024 by Nadia Gordynsky

All rights reserved solely by the author. The author guarantees all contents are original and do not infringe upon the legal rights of any other person or work. No part of this book may be reproduced in any form without the permission of the author.

Due to the changing nature of the Internet, if there are any web addresses, links, or URLs included in this manuscript, these may have been altered and may no longer be accessible. The views and opinions shared in this book belong solely to the author and do not necessarily reflect those of the publisher. The publisher therefore disclaims responsibility for the views or opinions expressed within the work.

Some names were changed to protect privacy.

Unless otherwise indicated, Scripture quotations taken from the Holy Bible, New International Version (NIV). Copyright © 1973, 1978, 1984, 2011 by Biblica, Inc.™. Used by permission. All rights reserved.

Paperback ISBN-13: 978-1-66289-356-8
Hard Cover ISBN-13: 978-1-66289-549-4
Ebook ISBN-13: 978-1-66289-357-5

TABLE OF CONTENTS

Chapter 1:   35,000 Feet in the Air 1

Chapter 2:   Growing up in Ukraine 9

Chapter 3:   It was our time 21

Chapter 4:   Gleams of the Future from
             American Pastor 35

Chapter 5:   When God opens the Door 49

Chapter 6:   Pieces of a Puzzle 59

Chapter 7:   God's Plan in Motion 63

Chapter 8:   When Everything Shuts Down,
             We Open Up 79

Chapter 9:   The War…Russian Invasion of Ukraine . . . 83

Chapter 10: Life and work during the war 95

Chapter 11: **LIFE or DEATH** 99

             Bio 103

Nadia Gordynsky's "Little Feet, Big Heart" is an excellent read! It will greatly encourage and inspire you to serve God in new ways. God gave Nadia a "God sized" vision and she is living out His plan for her life, even during extreme adversity with the ongoing, tragic war in Ukraine. The book starts with Nadia as a youngster and how she was radically transformed by the grace of God and incomprehensible power of the love of Jesus Christ! Incredibly interesting view of what is possible if you serve God with every ounce of energy that you have. Nadia is living out Colossians 3:23 to its fullest. My life was impacted by reading this autobiography! It makes you want to serve God even more. Nadia's ministry is having huge impact !!

Mark Whitacre, PhD.
(Vice President, Culture & Care for Coca-Cola Consolidated)

"Shortly after Russia invaded Ukraine, I learned of a seemingly fearless and certainly faith-filled pregnancy help leader supporting and starting pregnancy help centers in the chaos, confusion, and dangers of wartime. Similar to Esther in the bible, Nadia Gordynsky was clearly called by God 'for such a time as this.' And like Esther, she had to wrestle with the conditions before her and courageously step forward to help her people. Every page of this book carries her vision, her passion, her persistence, and her conviction to follow the Lord in saving lives."

Jor-El Godsey
President, Heartbeat International

INTRODUCTION

Dear Reader,

If you have this book in your hands, I want you to know that I am not an experienced writer. I don't even know if I am worthy of your attention or your time. I am not trying to teach you something new or impose my point of view on you. Since I remember myself, I always wanted to share what I have, what I experience with the people around me. Maybe it's not just me. Maybe it is the way God created us. He told Adam in the Garden of Eden: "It is not good for the man to be alone. I will make a helper suitable for him." (Book of Genesis, 2:18, NIV)

Yes, we need someone to share our life with, someone to experience what we experience, feel what we feel, taste what we taste.

Yes, here I am wanting to give you a taste of God's grace that I experienced. Feel the excitement of stepping into the unknown but known by God; taking the leap of faith and trusting that resources will come from God, the circumstances will align to accomplish a task when the woman in fear will look into your eyes and find hope and peace. I want you to travel to the foreign country of Ukraine with me, go back in time to experience of the fall of a tyrannical Communist Empire, explosion of evangelism and freedom of nineties in faraway places of the Soviet Union.

I want to share with you my heart-wrenching pain of losing my baby, a very private moments of my grief. Most of all I want to take you with me on the journey to witness the birth of the new organization with the noble mission from God to save the lives of unborn children.

Yes, I want you to join me on this mission....

> "Rescue those being led away to death,
> Hold back those staggering toward slaughter."
> (Proverbs, 24:11, NIV Bible)

DEDICATION

I am dedicating this book to the memory of my beautiful baby boy Johnathan, who came to this world to change my life. Although he lived only a short hour on this earth, his passing from this earth to Heaven transpired into over a thousand saved babies' lives and their mother's transformation.

I am grateful to my family for their love and acceptance and to my good friend Timothy K. Lynn for his consistent encouragement, ideas and that he made this book to become a reality.

Also, I am blessed with amazing family I call SALI.

Overall, My Daddy in Heaven who loves and cherishes me...

PROLOGUE

SEPTEMBER 2021

Save a Life International supports women in crisis. Our work emphasizes crisis pregnancy support, assistance to victims of violence and domestic abuse, and humanitarian aid for mothers and their children. We also educate young people about sexual integrity and the sanctity of life.

Six years after our first Life Center opened its doors in Chernivtsi, I am finally able to write how it all started. Ironically, I am on the train to Kiev from Kharkiv where our administrator Alla and I spent the last two days meeting the people. Over one hundred people came to hear about our ministry. Nastia and Denise met us at the train station and took care of us.

Pastor Anton, his young pregnant wife, and his team are full of fire for God! Will we have our seventh center here soon?

OCTOBER 2022

What is written above was my thought a year ago. Now the city of Kharkiv is in ruins from the Russian attacks. Hundreds of people are dead from artillery and bombs falling from the sky. Thousands fled the city and are now scattered all over Europe. The church where so many people worshiped God and came to hear our presentation is damaged too. The congregation is scattered throughout the country, living in refugee camps, in Europe, or in America. Pastor Anton was overseas when the war broke out. He hardly made it back in time to evacuate his wife and newborn baby boy.

My excited question a year ago, "Will we have our seventh center here soon?" was meant for the city of Kharkiv, the city I fell in love with on our trip last Fall.

God knew there would be a seventh center, but in another city and under different circumstances. Two months after the Russian bombs started to fall on Ukrainian cities and Russian soldiers brought death and destruction, our seventh Life Center opened its doors in the Western part of Ukraine. It became an oasis of love and security for those who had to flee for their lives. Just like all our Life Centers, it became a refuge place.

It also became our seventh center for pregnant women. These women were pushed to the brink of despair, so much so, that they were ready to get rid of their own flesh and blood through abortion.

The world had changed, our lives were forever changed.

Chapter 1

35,000 FEET IN THE AIR

"Life is sacred, and we must seek to protect all human life: the unborn child, the adult, and the aged."
— Billy Graham[1]

IT WAS 2007 and I was on the plane to Kiev. I left my two-month-old baby, Johnny with my husband Vlad and his mom. There was enough frozen breast milk in the freezer to last for nine days, after which I would return home. I was going to Kiev to take part in the crusade organized by the Billy Graham Association. I would be singing there on the main stadium in Kyiv, Ukraine. I was very excited, but I missed my baby. There were tears in my eyes when I thought of him.

Why was I there? I didn't know yet. I would know later. God would show me, but at that moment, I was there, in my country of birth that I left seven years before my loss.

---

[1] Billygrahamlibrary.org

The memory of the loss is still fresh in my mind to this day. The pain is still there for my little baby, Jonathan, who was born December 5, 2005. He was eighteen weeks old, still alive, but too small to survive a premature birth. My husband Vlad was with me in the hospital room when the baby was born after five days of doctors' efforts to stop my premature contractions.

"I am so sorry. There is nothing we can do. Your body is just rejecting the baby," the doctor said. "We can't stop the labor."

I didn't understand. I was healthy. The pregnancy was going well!

"*Why now? God, why now?*" I silently cried out.

After thirteen hours of labor, they told me to push. I knew the baby was coming, but there were no lights shining over my bed as it usually happens when a newborn is coming into this world. My baby was coming, but no one was expecting him to live. No lights were shining, no one was smiling to greet him. Just me, my husband, and the nurse were in the quiet room. After he was born, they asked us if we wanted to hold him.

"Yes, we do want to hold him, please," we told them.

The nurse brought him to us, and Vlad took him in his hands. Our little baby boy fit in the palm of his hand. His name was Jonathan. We had picked this name just a few weeks earlier. They wrapped him in a little blanket like a doll. I could see his little heart beating. My husband started crying. I could see him, I could hear what they were saying, but I didn't understand. It couldn't happen to me. It just wasn't real. It just was not happening to me. But, yes, it was real, and it happened to my husband, me, and our two girls.

***

Back to 2007. I got to Kiev, Ukraine. In the airport, I saw the familiar faces of Sasha and Danylo, my dear ministry friends from Ukraine, smiling at me. It was important to me to have someone meet me at the airport. I felt so small and unimportant, asking myself again what I was doing 10,000 miles away from my family and my newborn son, Johnny.

The crusade started two days later. I was ministering the first day. Then, I would meet with fans from the times when I lived in Ukraine and was a singer in the band "Svitanok" which my husband formed before we were even married.

We were quite popular in the late 80s early 90s. This was the time when the Soviet Union fell apart and Ukraine became independent. We traveled all over the former Soviet Union countries, singing at weddings, Christian concerts, and in many churches. I remember we were so poor, sometimes we didn't know what we would eat the next day, but we were so glad to serve God with our music freely, without any restrictions from the government.

BGEA Crusade in Kyiv, Ukraine 2007

Now, here I was in Kiev, singing my heart out on the biggest stadium in the country, and singing about Jesus—freely!

One day after the program, a young woman came to me backstage. Her name was Olga.

"Hi Nadia, remember me?" she asked. "I love your songs. I know them by heart! I live in Kiev now, work in the University, and am married with a little daughter. It would be wonderful if you could come back and perform in our town for the school kids. Would you do that? I feel we should start telling them about sanctity of life and how abortions are a plague in our nation."

Olga told me that abortion had become a form of contraception for women in Ukraine. During their eighteen years of independence, Ukraine lost 35-40 million babies to abortions. No one was teaching kids abstinence and parents themselves didn't even think abortion was the murder of innocent life. She told me about her own loss of a child, her pain, and how unfair it is when a woman who wants a baby loses the baby. At the same time and in the same hospital, there are women voluntarily letting doctors tear the child out of their wombs just because this baby was not wanted or comes at a wrong time in their life.

As we talked, more and more, we understood what we both stood for—our common passion for women in crisis.

GOD'S PLAN

When I came home from that trip, I thought I was going to return to my normal life, raising children, singing in the church, and my professional career. I thought I was returning to my nice, comfortable life in America.

Only that's not what happened! Day after day I thought about my birth country—Ukraine. I dwelt on the thoughts about the millions of Ukrainian boys and girls who had fallen as the victims of abortions, never getting a chance to take their first breath, cry their first cry, hear their mother's voice, feel their mother's comforting touch, and much more.

Seven months later, I was on the plane again. Only now I knew that somehow, I would be singing and sharing my story to help women and young girls realize how precious life is, even while that life is still in the womb.

That is how my Save a Life journey began. When I arrived in Ukraine, in May of 2009, my friend Olga organized meetings in the schools of Brovary. The host of the program was Eugene. He and his wife had taken in a two-year-old girl from an orphanage who survived an attempted abortion. She joined me on stage at the end of the program. Her name is Bogdanka and her story, which was shared on the local news, deserves to be known."

BOHDANKA'S STORY

Bohdanka's mother, a seventeen-year-old unmarried girl, came to the hospital five months pregnant and asked for an abortion. It is unbelievable to me that a doctor would perform a saline abortion at that stage of pregnancy but that was the reality of life in Ukraine at the time. The young woman was injected with a saline solution that was supposed to burn the baby. Then, labor was induced and when it was all over, she was discharged. No one told her the baby was still alive and moving during delivery.

The nurse didn't know what to do. She just couldn't bring herself to discard a living human being even though, by law, the baby was called an abortive material. She put the living, breathing child in the linen closet in hopes it would stop breathing on its own. Then with a clear conscience, she could discard it as biological waste.

After a few hours she came back to find that the little girl was still alive and moving. After informing the doctors about this extraordinary case, the baby girl was transferred to the new baby ICU unit recently purchased from the US.

For two years, Bohdanka lived in the hospital. She didn't walk and didn't talk. Everyone decided nothing good would come out of her life because she had a lot of complications and slow development.

Eugene and Marina visited the special unit for babies with defects quite often, bringing milk, clothes, and diapers. They decided to take Bohdanka into their own family. Doctors told them it was a bad idea, and she would never be a normal child, but they had made up their mind.

When I saw Bohdanka for the first time, she was four years old, holding her dad's hand, and shyly coming on stage to recite a short poem.

Bohdanka and I, 2009

Bohdanka and I, 2022

Chapter 2
GROWING UP IN UKRAINE

BEFORE MY DAD became a pastor, he was church choir conductor in another church for 20 years. Of course, he worked as a tailor to support his family because the church service was a volunteer position. In Ukraine at that time all work related with the faith and religion was not paid. Soviet government wouldn't tolerate it. Music was his passion and a way he served God. It was expected in our family to sing, but unfortunately my mom could only sing lullabies to her 8 children. Not all of us turned out to have an ear for music, but as for me, I was one of the siblings with a good voice.

And I sang! I loved to sing. Every night before going to bed my dad called all the family together for evening prayer. Before we would all get on our knees to pray, he usually said to me and my sister Galina: "Girls, come, let's sing!" Galina would sing with me and everybody else would start singing. My dad's favorite song was about the Good Shepherd who is looking for the lost sheep. At that time, my love for music was forming. Our church was very serious about music. The choir and orchestra had become the ways to express ourselves.

TWO WORLDS

For people who didn't grow up under the Soviet regime, it might be hard to understand how secluded the life of a Christian was in the country I grew up in. The Church was heavily persecuted in the Soviet Union and at that time, Ukraine was part of the Soviet Union. Any ideas of faith in God were considered old fashioned, dark, uneducated, and dangerous. We had to attend Soviet school where any religion was considered so called "opium for people", and if you believed in God the goal of the teacher was to "educate" you against your faith. So, if you were a child of Christian parents, you lived in two different worlds.

My family, 1980.

One world was that of a communist country, a regime that tried to brainwash people with all the attributes and believes of the Soviet government. Those attributes included: believing that God did not exist and that Christian parents were dark people. The only way to have a successful future was to leave your faith, follow the principles of communism, and show love and allegiance to your country leaders and embrace those values.

Another world was my family and my church. My parents had eight children. I was the seventh. From my earliest memory, God and the Christian faith were our life. Our mom taught us to pray. We grew up in church and used to be there almost every night participating in the different activities. All my friends were from church. I knew that I wouldn't be accepted among my school friends unless I embraced their values and beliefs (at least that is what I was taught by my parents). So, without even realizing it, we were growing up learning to live two different lives.

One life was true at home and another outside of home. This was necessary to survive in the country ruled by a godless government which was hostile to Christianity.

Reflecting, I now realize how damaging it can be for a person to grow in such an environment. I didn't know it then.

My class 4th grade.

    I was happy to live my life, play, sing, and hope for the future. Because my father was working full time in his tailor shop and serving in the church of 400 members as the pastor, he was never home, except those rare moments between work and church service, when he came home to eat and rest for an hour. The main burden of raising 8 children rested with my mother, and it took a toll on her very fast. She was often sick. To help my mother, my grandma took me in and would bring me home to our house every weekend until I started my 1st grade of school. My siblings sometimes teased me, although I don't think they were jealous, maybe a little bit, that I had my own room at my grandma's house, had my own toys, and my grandma's undivided attention. This was all while they were together, doing chores, and sharing the small living space with each other.

GRANDMA'S EXAMPLE

I was grateful for this time with my grandma Maria, who survived World War II.

She served on the front line as a cook for the soldiers, seeing death and destruction, losing her two husbands in the war, losing her baby only a few months after the birth, and living as a widow for the rest of her life. I remember her stories, told very hesitantly, about her war time. I loved to listen and was mesmerized by every detail. Her first husband, my grandfather Ivan, was a math teacher and he spoke seven languages fluently. When the war started, he was drafted right away, and she never saw him again. The news came that he was lost in action, and she became a young widow with two children, my mother and my uncle.

Devastated by the news, she left her son and daughter with her parents, who lived in the village close to the Dnipro River, joined the army, and was sent to the front lines. Here are some bits and pieces of her story in her words: "I left my unit and was wandering under the fire during air raids hoping to die. I didn't want to live. There was nothing for me to live for anymore after what I saw." She explained later that when her unit was retreating under the enemy fire to the other side of the Dnipro River, she saw her parent's village overtaken by fire and was convinced that her children and her family perished. But God had His own plan for her life.

My Grandma and me

I'll continue her story: "One time, there was something wrong with the food and many solders got sick. I was the one responsible for it, and it was considered sabotage. I had to be tried under the war tribunal and the punishment for sabotage was 10 years of labor camp or a firing squad. There was an officer who claimed that he loved me and wanted to marry me. At that time, I had already gotten the news that my husband Ivan was missing in action, which meant he was dead. Of course, I was grieving my husband that I loved and had two children with, but the reality of war and the bleak perspective of 10 years in labor camp that meant a death sentence, helped me to make my decision. It was the way out, and I took it."

Her marriage didn't last long. Soon, her second husband was killed in action and the baby girl that they had together during the war, died a few months after birth.

After the war was over, my grandma returned home and to her surprise and amazing joy she found her 2 children and her parents alive and waiting for her. She never remarried and after she met Jesus, her life was transformed completely. The rest of her life she dedicated herself to raising her children and serving people in need. She was an amazing example of service for me since I was a little girl.

I remember how my grandma used to take me with her to visit sick and elderly people who didn't have anyone and needed help. I remember one apartment where a young woman laid totally paralyzed, not able to move. Every couple of days we would go to her place. My grandma would wash her, change her clothes, feed her, and take home her dirty sheets to wash. I was 5 or 6 years old then and didn't understand much, but I saw my grandma take care of this lady with so much love. It is engraved in my memory until this day. The love of Christ was right there in front of my eyes, raw and sincere, without any strings attached or any glory or praise expected in return. It was just sacrificial and pure love, expressed by serving the least of this world.

What is serving? We were taught to serve, because Jesus served, but what is service to each of us? For some, service could be a way to justify our insecurity, to prove to ourselves that we are good. It could be the guilt for something unjust we have done in the past or maybe to win someone's approval. Maybe by serving others we want to compensate the lack of service or love in our life. It could be one or all these reasons. Or it could just be Love? Love that flows from a heart full of gratitude for the Love that was extended to us…

Recently, I heard one person dear to my heart tell me that his expression of love was his service to me. "I just want to serve you", nothing in return. True service goes hand in hand with love.

> **There is no other way, if it's not out of love, it becomes a burden, frustration, and just a bargaining chip.**

GOD KNOWS IN ADVANCE

***

If we really pay attention (most of us don't until something significant happens) to the amazing thread that God weaves in our lives, how many puzzle pieces He gently moves to create a picture of our life, we would be in awe!

***

But we don't pay attention, at least I didn't.

Every pain, every beautiful memory, every bright experience along with shameful ones form us into the person we are. And it works in the different stages of life too. As who we are as a person begins to form, our life may produce a specific fruit. Then as we grow, we may produce different fruit. God knows it all, and He is so gracious to use it all to prepare us for different stages. This is so we can accomplish His will and our purpose on this earth. This is what He did for me.

I didn't understand why when I was little, my dad played with me, but when I became a preteen, there was suddenly a big distance between us. The encouraging words suddenly turned into rebuke, disapproval, and "you're never good enough" cold silence. Now as an adult, I can assume that he just didn't know how to deal with me growing into womanhood. I was not a kid anymore, who he could throw in the air and tickle and laugh with!

I didn't understand why my elementary school gym teacher was suddenly looking at me differently from all other teachers, why he slowly started showing me special attention and telling me how special I was. I didn't understand until the abuse began. Any girl that has gone through the painful experience of being abused or taken advantage of will understand my feelings. She will understand what it means to feel so dirty and empty inside? Why couldn't I tell anyone about it? Why I felt special and at the same time wanted to die from shame? God only knew.

God knew that someday there would be another girl who would need to hear from older me, that she was not alone, that someone went through a similar experience, and felt the same pain, shame, and guilt. God knew there would be another girl who loved her father and was so dependent on his love, but never heard those life forming words, "I love you, my girl" from him.

What is it with the father? Why does a girl need him so much? Why does she need a man in her life that she can trust to protect her, defend her, and teach her to love. The lives of many women, unfortunately, will reflect their relationship with their father and form their opinion of men for the rest of their lives. That is a fact. There is no way around it.

GOD'S PREPARATION

As I mentioned before, the life of the Christian kid in my community revolved around church activities, music rehearsals, orchestra, Bible studies, and of course, the choir. When I turned 13, I was accepted to the main choir. Wow! It was a big deal! Of course, school activities, sports, and friends were an important part of my life, but anything I tried to do in school had to be secret from my dad, as he didn't want his kids to be involved in "worldly" activities. Sometimes it felt so unfair, and I believe it was, to keep his kids from exploring the world. We knew what we were allowed to do and what we were not allowed to do. For example, I was asked to be in the school plays and sing at the school concerts. But I was not allowed to participate, so I hid it from my dad. My mother was the most amazing, kind woman. She let us have our fun and kept it from our dad the best she could.

Now, being the mom of three children, I know how eagerly they want me to be present at their school plays, see their competitions, and cheer for them! And I did. My husband and I did everything possible to attend those events to support our kids.

But I raised my kids in America. They were different times. It was a different life. I didn't have the luxury as a child to have my parents cheer for me at my volleyball game or see me singing in the school choir. To American readers this could sound very strange, even cold. But it was a different life then, a different society, and a different world. Christians were separated from society or had to separate themselves to avoid losing their faith. But how do you explain this to the teen girl who wants to live, play, and explore the world.

I know that my parents did their best and raised us the best way they knew how.

***

I was born in Western Ukraine, near the Romanian border, and close to the border of Poland. Western Ukraine fell under the Soviet Union in 1939, while Central and Eastern Ukraine were under the Soviets 20 years earlier. As a result of this, Christian traditions were preserved longer in Western Ukraine than in Eastern Ukraine. That's why we knew that this was our time and mission to bring the Gospel to the rest of Ukraine and Russia.

At the beginning of the 1990s when the Soviet Union finally collapsed, freedom of religion came with it and many opportunities for bringing the Gospel to people were presented to us.

At that time in Russia, the protestant churches were almost non-existent. They were destroyed by the regime. So many of my friends joined the mission field and went to spread the Gospel in Russia.

Chapter 3

IT WAS OUR TIME

WE TRAVELED WITH our choir all over Ukraine, Russia, and Asia with evangelistic concerts. In the late 80s, early 90s people were so open to hear about God that all we had to do to was go to any town and set up a stage. Crowds of hundreds and thousands would come to listen. It was an amazing time of revival for the people who had been denied the access to religion and faith for 70 years of the communist rule. I remember every time after our concert, people would come forward, pray, and profess their faith in Christ. We would give them Bibles and talked with them. The world started to open for us! I joined the music band with my future husband, and we were touring all over the former Soviet Union countries, that at that time suddenly found themselves independent and open for the faith in God!

GOD'S PROTECTION

One of my first mission trip was to Yakutsk, Russia, a city located 280 mile south of the Arctic Circle. It is the coldest city in the world with an average annual temperature 17.6 F. The record low in winter was -83.9 F. We were flying there in April 1989 with a group of 12 singers and pastors, among which I was the youngest. I was 16 years old. Long flights, the time zone change, and many other economic factors made our trip very exhausting, but when you know your purpose, it makes everything exciting, especially when you are 16.

We were met by the local pastor missionary from Ukraine who started the small church a couple years ago in this city of 300,000. It was a small house with 2 rooms and contained 30-40 members. Imagine only small group of Christians for a city of 300,000?

BORSH ON THE ROPE

When we arrived, the pastor's wife told us that she would soon serve us Borsh (a Ukrainian soup). I followed her to the small kitchen expecting to see a big pot of Borsh on the stove. To my amusement, she opened a window and pulled a rope that was hanging out of the window. Then I saw a big chunk of red ice brought into the kitchen table, and she chopped a big piece of it and put it in the pot to warm up! The rest went back in the container, was hooked to the rope, and hung back from the window outside of the kitchen. That was our Borsh, and it was very good! And that was her freezer outside of the window for most of the year!

Our trip to Yakutia lasted for 3 weeks. We visited many concert halls, and a lot of prisons. Russia is known for its history of sending political prisoners and all who disagree with the regime to the prisons in Siberia. It is the most difficult and coldest climate in the world. During the 70 years of Communist rule, hundreds of millions of people died in labor camps in Siberia. The

Yakutsk region was one of those regions full of prison camps. And that's where we went with the Gospel of Christ.

Singing in Russian prison, 1989

Some of the following events are engraved in my memory forever.

INMATE WITH THE AMARYLLIS

We went to a men's prison outside of the city. In the main auditorium there were 200 prisoners listening to our singing and our message about Jesus. Being 16 was both an advantage and a disadvantage. I was so oblivious to the situation that I had no sense of danger. There were over 200 men with shaved heads, in striped robes sitting in front of the stage where our group was located, and almost no guards were around us. When my turn came to sing a solo, I stepped forward and started to sing. Suddenly, at the end of the auditorium, I saw a tall figure get up from the row and start to walk toward the stage. I don't remember anything in-between, but as I continued to sing. I then saw the big man standing in front of the stage with a big flowerpot and a red Amaryllis. Slowly, he stepped onto the stage and put his Amaryllis on the floor right at my feet. Later, he admitted that he was so moved by the Gospel of Christ, he wanted to show his gratitude by giving the flower that he himself raised in his cell.

WONDERING OFF INTO THE PRISON CELL

I have a wooden jewelry box beautifully carved, that sits on my bedroom chest of drawers. It is a nice piece of art reminding me of my youthful days. This was a gift from the prison sent to me 35 years ago after one of those missions trips. I don't really remember who it is from, but the letter of gratitude for our visit was there when I received it. It makes me think about how God used us to influence other people just by being present at the place where He wanted us. God knows, we don't. Maybe we'll never find out. He has His invisible hand over us when we are not even aware of the present danger, we are in.

One time, after our concert, the head of the prison in Yakuts invited us to join him for lunch. He was from Ukraine, and when he found out that we were from Ukraine, he was so excited to spend time with us. He left his land to join the Soviet Army and then moved to Russia to advance his career. Now, in his 50s, he ended up overseeing the big prison in Siberia, the coldest city in the world, thousands of miles from his homeland. Before the meal, while the tables were being prepared, he gave us a tour of the main facilities. I was walking and looking when suddenly, I realized I was way behind our group in a hallway with the many rooms. Here one man was talking with me, asking if he could show me his art made from plaster. We were in front of his cell, although it looked like a normal room, without any bars. "Come in, I want to give you one of my art pieces as a gift," he said, opening the door of his room. I stopped, looked around and realized that I heard the voices of our group very far in the distance. Not moving an inch, I stood there realizing how far they all were from me. This man wasn't part of the administration, he was an inmate, just in civilian clothes. I starting to think, "How can I get out? Where could I go?" And in a few moments, I heard the voice of Vasiliy, a group member calling my name.

I started to go toward his voice. There he was, turning the corner and saying with a big smile and relief in his voice, "Here you are! I realized you weren't with us and went looking for you!" And then I saw the rest of the group approaching, all was good. God watched over me when I didn't realize the danger, I was in.

There are many more situations when God showed His miraculous protection during our trips. It was amazing to speak with men and women who were in prison for 20-40 years. Some of them, when they heard the Gospel of Christ, remembered that their grandmothers were Christians and told them about their faith. It was a time of amazing movement of the Holy Spirit.

The hardest part for me was visiting women's prisons and the prison for boys. When I heard the story of a woman who was serving a long sentence for stabbing her husband who beat and raped her for years, I didn't understand much. I still judged her in my heart, thinking that she was a murderer. I didn't understand that she was the mother of 3 children who she left behind to be raised by a sick grandmother. I didn't understand the pain of not knowing what would happen with her babies and that it would be a long time until she could hug them again. I was only 16, what did I know? But God knew. He saw my life and the work I would be doing with those women many years later.

Those who grew up in Ukraine during the late 80s/early 90s will understand how unpredictable life was. Every day something changed. The Soviet Union was on the verge of collapse, the old ways of living didn't work anymore, but the new ways were not clear. The government tried to allow the new laws while keeping the old order from falling apart without any success. The "iron curtain" fell and people started to travel out of the country. They saw how the western world lived and the freedoms that other people had which had been denied to us for so many years. Big changes were in the air, and we lived through it. In the chaos there was uncertainty, but with the hope for the better future.

***

My wedding day was Saturday, August 3, 1991, and three days later we were on our way to the Crimea, the beautiful peninsula on the Black Sea. During the three weeks we spent there, we didn't listen to the radio and didn't watch television. But then, on the train home, we heard on the radio that there was a coup in Moscow, and General Secretary Gorbachev was held hostage on a ship in Crimea, just a few miles from the beach where we were. The country was in total chaos and nobody new how it would all end. Three days later, when we came home, the Soviet Union was no more. Ukraine had become independent and the economy and social order we grew up under were rapidly falling into the abyss.

An amazing thing happened though. We were allowed to travel out of the country! What an amazing surprise when our choir was invited to Germany, and we received visas! It was an unforgettable trip. It was the first time in my life I traveled outside of the Soviet Iron Curtain, to the western world, to Europe. I had read about it in books and had heard how the free people lived but I had not experienced it.

It is almost funny to remember how for the first time in my life I saw 5-10 kinds of the same product in the grocery store. So many kinds of cheeses, sausage, bread, candies, and more. We grew up knowing that in the store you can buy only 2 or 3 kinds of bread, 2-3 kinds of cheese and one kind of milk from the canister or in the bottle. I still remember walking into a shoe store looking around in wonder as if I was suddenly transported to a fairytale land! It was a new discovery and a new adventure for me and my husband to travel out of the country with our choir just 2 months after our wedding.

Sometimes, I wonder how fast human beings can adjust to the circumstances they are in. People are born to survive. How they survive depends on temperament, faith, family upbringing, and how they react to the situation they live in. For us, the main reason to look ahead in life was the chance to have the freedom. The freedom from Soviet Propaganda, the freedom to profess our Faith, and the freedom to choose our path in life!

And we lived it! Economically, it was very hard as prices of food increased 100%-300% in a few weeks. Sometimes, we didn't know where we would buy food for the next day, standing many hours in line to get milk or bread. The meat was a luxury! Even if we could afford to buy it, we still had to stay in long lines to get it.

Our first daughter Olesia was born 2 weeks before my 19th birthday. I was still a child myself holding in my arms this beautiful baby girl with big blue eyes and puffy cheeks. I don't know what I would have done if not for my mom! When I came home from the hospital (I don't wish giving birth in a Soviet style hospital on anybody), my husband had to go on a tour with our church orchestra for the Evangelistic Crusade. Yes, I moved to my parents' apartment until he was back a couple weeks later. What a precious gift of a mother, especially my mother! She took care of me completely while I was recovering from birth. I'll never forget and never undervalue the help she provided for me. Most of all, it was unconditional love that only mother can give.

GIFT OF A MOTHER

Each of us had been given a gift of a mother.

With my mother, 1998

I miss my mom. Her name was Luda. No matter how much time passed since l last saw her, hugged her, felt the warmth of her embrace, I desperately need her to just be around. Those are the moments when I feel lonely, when things don't go the way, I planned. I miss the encouraging spark in her eyes, that would mean "Go on, girl! All will be alright!". I don't remember her sad or angry. When things got hard, and most of her life was hard for her, she never lost her optimism, her joy and zest for life.

My mother's childhood was stolen by the World War Two. Both of her parents were drafted and after a short time her dad was killed in action.

She and her brother were left with the grandparents under the German occupation. How they survived the occupation was pure God's providence.

She was telling me that when Germans came into the village, they threw their family, grandparents, her and her brother Vova from their house, took away the cow, which was the main source of their food. They had to live in the hole in the ground that was made as a cellar to store the produce throughout the winter. Grandpa Kostya used his masonry skills to make this cellar acceptable for living and that is how they were prepared to live. The German soldiers lived in the house. My mom was 6 and her brother was 8 years old.

She was telling how she remembers one solder that was stationed in their house made her brother pick some straw for the horses. Little Vova was trying to do what he was told and was piling up the straw. Suddenly the wind started to blow, and all the pile was blown away before the horse got to it. The angry solder started to hit the boy with his rifle, the boy fell on the ground, covering his head with the hands. Suddenly someone grabbed the solder and dragged him away from the boy. Then the blow in the face followed and my mom said that it was another German, their sergeant. Little Vova was saved from the beating by the other German. Later, she remembered that this man apologized to her grandmother Haritina for the incident and told her using broken Russian that he doesn't want this war. He said that he left 2 little children and his wife back home and he misses them a lot. He said that his children are the same age as my mother and her older brother. From that time on he was secretly giving them the food so they wouldn't die from starvation.

All the terrible things she experienced as a child, being an orphan, surviving the post war years and a lot of hardship didn't make her bitter or depressed. She was the most resilient women I ever met in my life. She had to raise 8 children, work and hosted a lot of different people who visited our family all the time.

Being the pastor's wife and a mother of 8 children was hard on her, but I never heard a word of complaint or accusation. She loved to read the books whenever she could, especially when we grew up and she had more time, she always shared about her new book that she read. I could write the whole book about this amazing woman's life, but now I can only feel the tightening pain in my chest and realization of how much I need her now. I am grateful for the gift of my mother, even only for a short 24 years of my life.

***

Each puzzle piece has its own role in the big picture of life.

***

As I mentioned before, my mother and her brother survived during World War II because one German officer, the enemy and occupier was feeding them in secret from his own fellow soldiers. God miraculously took care of my mother even through the enemy and was weaving the story of the next generation. The same divine intervention happened to my father's family.

MIRACLES THAT FORMED THE DESTINY OF THE NEXT GENERATION

Recently I visited Ukraine and this time I was at the grand opening of our new Life Center in the city of Rivne, where my father's family is from. Some of my cousins are still living in the villages on the outskirts of Rivne. This time, I was determined to get them together at least for one dinner. To my joy, we had a wonderful dinner together with the three of them. We reminiscent about our childhood years, our parents, and grandparents.

During that dinner, I found out this story. My dad Peter was the second oldest in the family of 10 children. His father, my grandfather, Anton was fighting in the war and my grandma Yulia was left with the small children. When German SS soldiers were burning the villages around the city of Rivne, they came to the village where my grandmother lived with her children. The soldiers started going from house to house looking for the people. My grandmother was hiding with children in the cellar. My uncle Stepan was a little baby at that time, and he started to cry. Of course, the soldiers found them and told them to come out of the cellar. One by one all the children and my grandmother were out of the cellar and were told to go in the house. Praying to God as it was their last moments before certain death, they obediently went into the house and a soldier went in with them. Suddenly, he saw the words from the Bible written on the wooden plank hanging on the wall.

It said, "But as for me and my household, we will serve the Lord" Joshua 24.

The soldier stopped, looked at my grandmother Yulia, and asked, "Do you really live according to those words?" he asked. She answered, "Yes, we do." Then he turned to the other soldiers that were with him ready to burn the house and said, "Let's go. We won't do anything to them," and they left. That day the only house that was spared from the fire was my grandmother's house. The rest of the village was set on fire and burned down.

It is amazing how every detail in our lives matters. Each puzzle has its own role in the big picture of life. God carefully taking care of every situation and using it for His great purpose. When I think of this, I want to fall to the ground in awe and worship our Creator.

Chapter 4

GLEAMS OF THE FUTURE FROM AMERICAN PASTOR

Some circumstances or events in our lives can be so hard to explain or interpret until many years later.

Growing up in a conservative Baptist church, the prophecies or voice of God would seem strange to a common person. When I grew up and someone would claim God clearly told them something, we would just smile and sometimes roll our eyes.

In the mid-nineties, our music band was invited to participate in an evangelical outreach organized by American missionaries. We would sail on the cruise boat and every day we would dock at the major cities along the Dnipro River. From Kyiv, the Dnipro flows through a picturesque mountain landscape and cuts into the reservoir above Zaporizhzhya City. Below Zaporizhzhya, the Dnipro enters the steppe belt, the dry Black Sea Lowland. Later, it enters a wide valley and in the final stretch near Kherson, it splits into branches and forms a large delta with numerous islands and lakes. The lower Dnipro past Kherson flows straight into a Black Sea near Odessa. We were privileged to see and enjoy all this beauty of the Ukrainian landscape and on the top of this, we got to spread the Good News of the Gospel to the people who lived in those cities along the Dnipro River.

There were 200 Americans on the boat and around 50 Ukrainian pastors. One sunny day I am sitting on the deck enjoying the warm sun. Suddenly, I heard a voice behind me. It was a pastor from Chicago. He turned to me and said, "God wants me to tell you something." I didn't know how to react. It was so foreign to me! Why would God speak with anyone about me!? With a smile and some skepticism in my voice I said, "Sure, tell me." It was shocking to hear from him all the details about my life and the situation I was in at that time. He even told me about the state of my soul. I met this pastor for the first time in my life and never planned to see him again. I was stunned. He went back to his chair, but after a few minutes he jumped out of it and asked if he can tell me more of what God told him.

This time I was not skeptical anymore. I listened with reverence and some fear. He said, "Nadia, I know you are going through hard times right now. There will be dark days and valleys ahead of you, but eventually you will be influencing many and God will use you in the big way. Some day you will be traveling all over the world with the message of His Hope". I don't remember word for word, but I remember the message he conveyed to me.

Me? The girl from the small town in the third world country that was recently out of darkness of communism. It was so unreal, so hard to believe. And to tell you the truth, I didn't believe it until many years later when I found myself on the other side of the world, in a different society, in different circumstances. God had been giving me hints, little glimpses, but I didn't see it, why would I? Right?

> **How often He so gracefully sends us a small signal, asking us to be courageous, showing us the future that we refuse to accept and believe in.**

NEW LIFE IN AMERICA

The changes were coming fast. Two years later I was on a plane to New York with my 5-year-old daughter, and I was 6 months pregnant with our second baby girl. We were going to join my husband who went to America earlier to start a new life in a new country. It was winter 1998. I remember the ride from New York to Philadelphia, where we were going to make our home. Everything was frighteningly huge. The roads seemed very wide, the buildings very tall, and the roads too long. America, the land of opportunity was welcoming us to start brand-new life. Everyone who immigrated to the new country had their own story to tell.

My story was not as easy as I dreamed. Three months later, 3 weeks before the birth of our daughter I received the horrible news. The phone call came from Vlad, my oldest brother from Canada. He was crying. Our mom had a heart attack, and she was dead. My mother, who I was hoping to bring to America soon, to help me with my new baby. My mom, who was my light, my rock, the closest person to me in the world. I was only 24.

It was too early, too tragic, too sad. My world collapsed, and I was lying in bed for 3 days looking at the ceiling, unable to fly to Ukraine for her funeral. I didn't realize that my last "Goodbye" 3 months ago was really my last. I had to go on. I had to be strong for my daughter and another one, who was just about to be born. We called her Luda, my mother's name. One life went away, and another came to this world. It was the circle of life. God is in control of it all.

LORA: GOD PAVES THE WAY

When you think your life is settled, you have children, a job, a house, friends, and a church you really like, something extraordinary happens and your reaction to the situation can determine your readiness for your new chapter in life. Only you still have no idea. The pieces of your life's puzzle are still coming together one by one to form a beautiful picture. You just don't know where those pieces will come from. Sometimes they come one by one, sometimes they are just thrown at you by the bunches.

When Johnny, my baby boy, was 6 months old I decided to go to work in a clothing store two nights a week. I worked in the clothing boutique and enjoyed interaction with women. I loved to pick the right outfits and make the women feel beautiful. It was so special to put a few pieces of clothing together, and then see the customer feel so grateful and beautiful walking out of the boutique with the smile. It was one of my easiest and pleasant jobs!

One night a couple came to our store and with them there was an older woman. It was the husband's mother. The mother evidently was the most confident one. She went straight to me and asked if I could make her daughter-in-law look good. When this woman heard my accent and figured out that I could speak Russian, she became even more insistent. I looked at her daughter-in-law and said, "I think she is beautiful and doesn't need help, but if she wants to look at something I will be glad to show her what we offer." The young woman's name was Lora, and she looked at me with gratitude and a hesitant smile showed on her pretty face. I could tell that she was clearly intimidated by her mother-in-law. She thanked me, and we started to talk.

Lora came to the states from Belarus as a student and then married her husband, Jon who was a student from Ukraine. At that time, he was a resident in the hospital, and she was working to support his school study. The plan was when he got a job as a doctor, she would go to school to become a nurse. That's how we became friends. They visited us occasionally, and Lora started to open up to me as her older sister, because her family was in Belarus, and she practically had no family. Lora and Jon grew up in communist countries, and God was something foreign to both of them. Slowly we started to talk about God and faith, and they knew that we loved God and were always willing to talk about our faith.

Then we heard the news they were pregnant. We were so glad to hear it, but sensed the strange vibe coming from Jon. He didn't seem to be that excited. Time went by. One night, I got a phone call. It was Lora crying on the phone. at first, I couldn't understand what she was talking about, but later it started to make sense.

She called me from the gas station and told me that her husband brought her to a clinic for an abortion. He didn't tell her about it until they arrived there. She said that he had already made her have an abortion before, but this time she refused. And now she had no idea what to do next. Honestly, I had no idea how to react, but one thing I knew for sure was she needed me to tell her what to do. And I did. I told her that she could come to my house and stay with us as long as she needed. And that there was no way she could let her baby die. She would fight for him! She would keep this baby alive.

Eventually, she moved in with us, as her husband started to build his life without her. There were a lot of things happening during her pregnancy, but baby boy was growing in her belly. When the time came, my husband and I took her to the hospital where little Sasha was born. What a joy it was for me to hold him in my arms. I didn't know what to call myself, auntie, or grandma. Lora and Sasha lived with us for a while until they found a place of their own. After Sasha was born his parents divorced, but his father had come to love him and was proud to have a son. I was so blessed to visit Lora and Sasha until they moved to Belarus.

Years passed by and I hoped to see them sometime. When pregnant Lora came to live with us, I had just started to visit Ukraine with the message of life, working with the students, and teaching them about the sanctity of life. I didn't think that someday I would dedicate my life to saving babies like Sasha from abortion. I didn't know, but God knew! I didn't realize but God was already testing and preparing me for my life's work. He was teaching me to love not just with words but with the deeds. It was one thing to talk about abortion and another to be ready to do something about it, to get out of a comfort zone, and to love in practice.

One of such an expression of love for the expectant mothers was my song that was written soon after God sent pregnant Lora on my path.

> You are walking alone down the road, looking nowhere
> Tears glisten in the eyes, a stone is weighting heavy on your heart
> You know the Life is already beating inside, and quietly someone is whispering to you
> I am here, alive, have mercy, Mother, let me live
>
> The life that is in you is defenseless, the choice is given to you
> And the voice is speaking in your heart, Mother, let me live
>
> How terrible it is to never hear that first cry in the quietness of night
> The warmth of a defenseless heart that would warm your soul
> How painful it is to know that you never will hear the laughter
> that gives you Your the most precious baby, that you are about to destroy
> Years pass quickly, the life flies away like a short moment
> That voice that you despised and rejected still pierces your heart,

That voice is sweet and scary, does sound like a verdict for you
That's the same voice of your child continue to whisper: Mother, let me live

Our first babies saved from abortion with their moms, 2016

VISION OF THE SAVED CHILDREN

Why do we have to go through pain? I hear often that pain soften our hearts, makes us vulnerable and sensitive. The famous phrase, "what doesn't kill you makes you stronger" doesn't agree with me. The pain can make you stronger but can also break or damage you for the rest of your life. It depends on what is holding you through the pain, who do you trust to support you or to love you through the process? What do you hope to see ahead?

When my husband and I were in that hospital room holding our first baby boy, the pain was excruciating. Nothing made any sense! I didn't want the pain to make me stronger. I wanted my baby alive! I wanted the pain to go away. At that time, I didn't think about what was ahead of us or how God would use it for the benefit of others. Sometimes we need time to figure this out and sometimes He gives us encouragement in an extraordinary way. To tell you the truth, I didn't believe in visions much. When I heard people say that they had a vision it sounded like arrogance to me until I experienced it myself. I still remember it very clearly, 16 years later.

One of my daily routines is jogging in my neighborhood. It was a beautiful summer morning, and I was walking fast to catch my breath after a mile of running. I didn't close my eyes, I just walked, but suddenly I saw heaven cut in half horizontally. I was below and at my eyes level I saw a figure standing surrounded by children in white. They were all different ages and different heights. I looked up and immediately knew that it was Jesus. With a heart full of gratitude, I reached up from where I was standing and wrapped my arms around Jesus's feet. I will never forget the feeling of overpowering love, gratitude, and joy when I touched His feet. I was grateful for the privilege to save these children's lives. I knew somehow that they were our children, saved from abortion.

I can't explain how I knew…. Save a Life was just getting off the ground then.

Suddenly, everything disappeared, and I was still walking. I was in another place, maybe a quarter of a mile ahead. It happened to me! I knew it was not a dream! I saw Jesus's figure and children so clear! I still can't get it out of my head even now. Perhaps never. God gave me the sign; He showed me the future! He showed me that my pain was worth it. As I write this, over one thousand children have been saved, and the first one, little Timothy, went to the first-grade last fall.

JUNE 2, 2023

I am again 35 000 feet in the air. Again, I am writing on a plane. It looks like all 'important' chapters of this book are born on a plane, in the air, far from the ground, and closer to heaven. Last week I turned 50. What a milestone!

I know that God has a plan for my life. He already knows what will happen as it already happened, but I don't. All I can do is just to live day by day, making the decisions I am meant to make, some are the wrong ones, but I am trying to make the right ones. I am learning every day to trust God, even if it hurts like hell! My flesh doesn't want to be denied of its pleasures and its "wants". My soul is listening to the Spirit of God. Who is going to win today, flesh or spirit? It is a constant war between flesh and spirit, and we all carry our battle scars. I am learning not to dwell on my past losses, but trust God's promise that I am His bride, His princess that He died for. The flesh wants me to feel guilt, pain, shame, and regrets. The Spirit whispers gently, "Nadia, you are enough. You are my daughter. You are loved."

I am so grateful for a few people that God sent on my path who are constantly and lovingly saying those words to me. I get up with a smile of gratitude and joy making small steps toward the victory, happiness, and peace.

DECISION TIME

Ever since the first trip to promote sanctity of life with Olga and the team in Brovary, Ukraine on May 2009, my pro-life journey has continued. I started traveling with my team all over Ukraine, visiting schools, and universities with the message of life, telling my story. It was amazing to watch how God sent me the right people at the right time and in the right place. I remember after speaking in church about my upcoming trip to Ukraine, one girl came to me and told me straightforward, "Nadia, I want to go with you! I will do anything you want me to. I will carry your bag, assist you, just take me with you!" Yes, Alla, went with me, but she didn't have to carry my bag. She was an amazing support. She could speak with the girls after the presentations, she prayed with me after a long day in the hotel room, and she gave me suggestions and emotional support. Now she is a very successful mother of two girls and a joyful pastor's wife. God was slowly filling our team with great musicians, doctors, and speakers and in a few years, we were invited to academic institutions all over the country. I don't even remember how I picked the right people for our talk show. God was sending old friends with talents for different things. We were perfecting our presentation every year with the key musician Ivan, who was the lead singer of a famous Christian band in Ukraine at that time.

I remember the Dean of the University of Khmelnitsky called us into the President's office and was telling the President how effective our message was and how relevant it was to the students.

She said, "Every year I have to deal with a few pregnant girls on the campus, and I am sure that many girls just quietly go through with an abortion. Later, we deal with suffering, depressed young women who can't go on with their lives, because of what they have done. We need to educate our students about the consequences of premarital sex and the truth about the consequences of abortion. This team was holding the student's attention to the very end, and I saw the emotion on their faces! These presentations can save someone's life and will definitely prevent some abortions."

For six years our ministry was expanding, and I was traveling overseas more and more often. It had become harder to work full time and travel as all my time off was dedicated to travels to Ukraine and spreading the message of life everywhere we went. Meanwhile, I was educating myself on pregnancy care, counseling, and everything that would equip me to be productive and useful. I was getting to know more people who cared about the plague of abortion, but surprisingly, nobody openly talked about it in Ukraine except us. I realized that there were only a few pregnancy care centers in the country, and they were started by American missionaries. It seemed like everybody knew about abortion, but no one was willing to talk about it. Christians hardly heard it from the pulpits in evangelical churches. It was a taboo issue, very hush hush and even shameful to mention in public. The more I spoke with people there, the more I realized that this was the time and place to bring it to the light!

God was slowly nudging me, whispering, and sometimes loudly speaking to me through some people in my life.

I have to give credit to the dear Pastor David Bentley. He ministered in Ukraine for many years, serving women and children and bringing up the issue of abortion among Christians and medical personal. He came to Ukraine in the early 90s and started to visit hospitals, offering some medical supplies which was so needed at that time. He probably was the first missionary to Ukraine after the fall of the Soviet Union who openly brought the issue of abortion to light. Because of him, many beautiful children are walking this earth, and their mothers are happy to have them. In May 2015 during one of the pro-life retreats in the Carpathian Mountains, that he organized, David asked me to help with the program and do some training courses on communication. I was glad to meet women and men with the same passion for the unborn. At that time, there were probably 30-40 people from different parts of the country, and they all were united by the same desire to bring awareness about abortion in Ukraine and learn how to be affective in pro-life movement.

One day while sitting in the log cabin with David, I expressed my grief over the millions of children killed by abortion in my home country. In return, David looked at me and said with a smile on his face, "Nadia, stop whining and mark the day in your calendar when you have your first board meeting and create your own organization." Stunned, I looked at him in amusement. "Who? Me? What do I know about founding a charity?" That day we prayed together in that little room in the middle of the mountains and the seed was planted. God slowly (maybe not that slowly) started to work in me. That day I chose a date in my mind: September 23 and four months later four of my friends including my husband were sitting in our dining room, signing the memo that started the Save a Life International.

To the reader it might sound so simple. It sounded simple even to me sometimes when I look back, but it wasn't. I came back that May from Ukraine and shared this idea with my husband Vlad, although he was supportive, I was scared. Suddenly, I realized that I must educate myself in many areas of pregnancy counseling, learn about the non-profit world, and most of all quit my career. I had a good job that I enjoyed and financial security. Now I had to make the leap of faith and journey to the unknown. God was working on my heart, teaching and gently encouraging me even when I was arguing with Him. I remember sitting on my back porch crying, crying, and crying… not understanding why I felt so lonely and lost. That's when God started speaking to me through Psalm 119. Day by day I was reading the same chapter and every word, every lament of David, every complaint, and every praise was echoing in my heart. I was changing, my life was changing.

Chapter 5
WHEN GOD OPENS THE DOOR

When God Opens the Door, He Keeps it Open Until the Room Fills up with the Right People.

IT IS AMAZING to watch how one phone call can cause a ripple effect and the Holy Spirit brings people you totally forgot were in your life in the past to you. I called my old friend who is a pastor in one of the churches in my hometown Slavik. I mentioned that I am doing presentations in Ukrainian schools with my team talking about sex, love, relationships, as they relate to abortion and sanctity of life. I mentioned my own personal loss of my son, Johnathan. After hearing what I had to say, I heard his voice full of enthusiasm: "Nadia! This is exactly what we were looking for! We need a ministry like this. Please, come and speak at our church, and I will invite those who are interested to come to hear you speak."

Then I had a conversation with some other friends who I knew from my youth, Sasha and Ira Utkin. When I lived in Ukraine and worked in the TV studio for a few years as a producer of Christian programs, Sasha and Ira were the young couple who I interviewed for my program. I remember it like it was yesterday. They were just two teenagers, the guy with the long hair and his shy girlfriend who had just come to Christ through the Young Life Camp. Full of excitement and the desire to serve the Lord, they were sharing their story in front of the camera in my studio. That is how I remembered them, but when someone suggested to invite Sasha and Ira to see our presentation in Ukraine and invite them to be our partners, I didn't know that Sasha had been heading Young Life Ministry in Ukraine for 20 years by then. I saw them as young teenagers 20 years ago and now I hardly recognized them, especially Sasha! Yes, we all changed. Our lives took their own turns. We all had different times of loss, grief, and joy. Now Sasha and Ira had 6 kids and a big Young Life ministry to run. I came back from the US with my own story, trying to start a new ministry that not many people in Ukraine were familiar with. At that time, I had no big supporters, no funds, but a lot of faith, enthusiasm, and many friends, who loved God and were willing to serve. What a treasure we have in our Christian family. The blood of Jesus and His amazing grace put us in a special category of God's family, and it is more than any family can provide.

After my conversation with David Bentley back in May 2015, we visited Sasha's and Ira's house where they had gathered women and men who wanted to hear about pro-life ministry in the US. David was very good at bringing up the abortion issue and the importance of such a ministry. I was listening to him at Utkin's house and was convinced more and more that God was calling me to do this work.

I will never forget the words Sasha told me when I shared my vision with him. "Nadia, I will give you one room in our Young Life headquarters building free of charge. I will help you in any way I can, just do everything you came here to do to make sure that the blood of innocent children will never be shed because of lack of knowledge and support."

And he did keep his word. We set the date, October 30, 2015, to open our Life Center in one of the rooms of the Young Life building in the city of Chernivtsi, my hometown.

The time had come to travel to Ukraine to open our First Life Center.

Sometimes it is a blessing to be oblivious to the difficulties of starting something new. It is like a brand-new wife who is pregnant and very excited to have the baby. She has no idea what it means to go through the labor. She doesn't yet know how much pain she will have to endure until the beautiful little human will be put on her chest, often crying and not happy to see the bright lights of the delivery room. The baby is crying and that is a sign of life, and as for the mother, she forgets her pain with the one glimpse and touch of this little thing, which minutes ago had been causing her excruciating pain. All is forgotten, the joy is here.

My labor pains had just started when I came that October to my hometown. I was introduced by Pastor Slavik to his church called "Grace". During Sunday morning service I was given an opportunity to sing my songs and speak about my intention to open the center to help abortion minded women to make the decision for life for their babies. After that, I invited anyone who was interested in being a volunteer in this new ministry to come Sunday night and hear more about the training that we would start on Monday. Sunday night we had no idea if anyone would come but by 5pm 34 people had shown up. I started our Sunday night gathering by praying with everyone for God's guidance in every step and every decision we were about to make. Yes, it might sound strange and reckless to move that fast, but I had to trust God for His provision and guidance in every little detail.

After introducing the idea and the structure of the future Life Center, I asked all who would like to go through the pregnancy counseling training next week to fill out the application with the questionnaire, clear their nights for the next week, and be ready to show up for the training next Monday evening at the Young Life headquarters conference room.

Also, our "Sanctity of Life" school presentation team was arriving the same Sunday night, and we were about to start our presentations in Chernivtsi's schools on Monday morning. We would do two shows a day until Friday, the day we had scheduled our Life Center opening. All was supposed to work simultaneously: presentations in schools during the day and trainings of the new team of volunteers at night.

By Friday morning we planned to select up to 12 volunteers for the team. The leader, a Christian woman who was a medical nurse was picked out ahead of time, and I was confident that she could lead the team. Of course, something had to go wrong, and it did, or at least so I thought. After a long conversation with our chosen leader, we realized that she wouldn't be able to lead the team, and we had to have a plan B. We didn't have one. I remember sitting with Sasha, Ira, and my team scratching our heads. What are we going to do now? Then Paul, our presentation team leader and dear friend said, "Guys, we don't have a choice but to trust God to show us the new leader. Let's pray and trust Him to show us the woman who will be willing to do this work."

To tell you the truth It wasn't an easy choice for me. I like to solve problems, manage, organize, and keep things under control. God was teaching me another lesson. So, it was agreed by Wednesday night to pick the candidate from the collected applications and choose our leader. Hmmm, easy task, right?!!!!

THE WOMAN, WILLING TO SERVE.

Wednesday, after a long day of presentations in the local university to a couple hundred students and a long night of training, we finally set down at the kitchen table in Utkin's house. It was past midnight, but no one was sleepy. We reached out to the fridge and started pulling out night snacks: some beckon (traditional Ukrainian fat), bread, honey, and cheese. Of course, nothing could be eaten without tea, traditional herbal tea. Now we could read through the applications and choose our team leader.

Slowly, I was going through each application. Nothing caught my eye, so I prayed, "Lord, please guide me. Give me the discernment that I need."

And He brought her to me.

Mila Zarubaiko was serving as a missionary in Rwanda for a year and a half. She came back from Rwanda to be with her friend Dina, who was about to have a baby girl. Mila explained to me later. "Last week Dina delivered a stillborn baby girl. I was with her and her husband, trying to comfort them, but I didn't know how. With my effort to get her out of the house, I asked her to come with me to the church where you gave your presentation. She didn't want to see anyone, but I insisted, thinking it would help her to be with the people. After the presentation we were introduced by my mother to you, and she told you about Dina's loss. You wrapped your arms around Dina and told her that you understand her pain. You asked her if she named her baby girl. You were present and loving and paid attention. I didn't even know why but we decided to come to the training. Maybe hoping that it would help me to understand how to comfort my friend? Maybe it would help her through the grieving process."

Yes, I knew Mila's parents! I remembered her as a little girl. I and her mother Zhenia were in one church and my oldest daughter Olesia and Mila were only a year apart. Memories had been coming back to me about my life in Ukraine, going to the church, and playing with our babies outside of the church during the service.

The voice inside of me was telling that she was the one I had to ask. Tomorrow night during the coffee break I would ask. "Thank you, Lord. Now it is up to You to deal with Mila's heart," I prayed.

Thursday our team had one presentation in a local school and our training started as usual. The same people that attended the day before filled up the room ready to listen. The first part of the evening went smoothly, and I was going to approach Mila during the coffee break and invite her for lunch the next day. At lunch, I was going to offer her the Life Center Director position. Also, on that Friday at 6 o'clock in the evening we had scheduled the grand opening of our center. You might think it was crazy and irresponsible to do this all in such a short time and so simultaneously. I agree. But back than it seemed so simple and logical. I knew God was working in all of this, and it gave me peace.

While I was getting ready to approach Mila, I noticed her walking slowly towards me. She leaned over the desk I was sitting at and hesitantly said, "My name is Mila, and I just came back from Rwanda, where I was serving for a year and a half. I am thinking of going back as soon as my friend Dina recovers, but meanwhile I want to offer my services. You can use me in the new center any way you want. I can wash the floors, clean, and help with anything that needs to be done. I am willing to volunteer, because I live with my parents, and I won't have to look for a job.

I was stunned! Really? Here is your answer, Nadia!

Friday, our ribbon cutting ceremony was scheduled for 6 pm and here we are, sitting in the restaurant at 12 pm, 6 hours before the opening. "Mila, I would like to ask you to lead this new team that we just selected. If I ask you to be a director for at least 3 months until we find somebody else. Would you do it?"

She looked at me and without thinking for too long said, "Yes, I will. Although, I have no idea why you picked me, but if you say so, I will." Six hours later she was serving the drinks and sandwiches at our Life Center opening.

Next day I went back to America with the promise to return in a month. I left Mila with 12 volunteers, training manuals, instructions on how to run the center and a $300 budget. That was all the money I had at that time, but I had a lot of faith. The help line was working, and we had a billboard in the city with our phone number on it and a big picture of a girl and the words "Lost and pregnant? Don't know what to do? Call us! We can help". I left, but Mila stayed.

She worked and learned and worked again. She had become my right hand, my helper, and my friend. I have to admit that Mila wouldn't function and do what she did without her best friend Dina. Yes, the same Dina who lost her baby girl a few days before our training started and the reason Mila came to us. That is how we started to build Save a Life. Three girls, dreaming together, brainstorming, and strategizing together. These two young girls in their mid-twenties had become my pupils, my daughters, and our first employees. I was so blessed to watch them both absorb all I was teaching them. Especially, we were at our best when we prayed for guidance from God and each other.

I will never forget those first years when we traveled on trains or by van from city to city, speaking in the churches, sharing the vision God gave us and building the new teams for the future Life Centers in Ukraine.

Mila, Dina and I, 2017

Our first Life Center team, 2015

Chapter 6
PIECES OF A PUZZLE

It is April 2023. I am holding in my hands our first professional Save a Life International Impact Report. It is a beautiful, colorful book printed on glossy paper. Thanks to our amazing designer Ben it looks fabulous! But my eyes are focusing on the happy face of the 7-year-old boy, captured in a running motion on the front cover page. His name is Timothy and the smile on his face is so bright, open, and full of determination and zest for life! He is going to the first grade!

Baby Timothy going to school

It is almost impossible to imagine that this smile might have never happen, that there wouldn't be the first-grade experience, no running, no life… There wouldn't be the boy, wouldn't be Timothy walking on this earth…if his mom would have gone through with what she was going to do. At four months pregnant she had a referral for an abortion. She was a teenage runaway. Her name was Yulia.

MANY PIECES OF ONE PUZZLE TO FORM A BEAUTIFUL PICTURE OF LIFE. YULIA STORY.

Yulia was our first client.

Three weeks after the opening of our Life Center, Mila received the phone call. There was a young girl's voice on the other end. "Is this Life Center? My friend is pregnant, and she has a referral for abortion, but I wanted to see if maybe you can help," the voice said.

Yulia showed up an hour later with her friend Elisa. They both were surprised how welcoming Mila was. She offered them some tea and cookies and waited until Yulia calmed down and loosened up a little bit. She told Mila that she had a nine-month-old baby boy named David in the village where she lived with her stepfather, mother and 4 more children. She was the oldest. She didn't share who the father of her baby was. All she wanted was to get rid of this pregnancy, somehow take her baby David from her parent's house, and live as far away as possible from them. There was a lot to uncover, but Mila knew that right now Yulia needed help, and she was in the right place.

After the long conversation, which included showing her little plastic models of babies at different stages of development, Yulia decided to keep the baby. She asked if someone from our Center could go to her village with her and help her to get her son from her parents. She was so scared to face them alone. Mila and a couple of volunteers agreed to go. It was a very interesting trip, which involved a lot of drama and a lot of convincing. We agreed to help her find a place to live in the city, help her during the pregnancy, and help after the baby was born, until she was on her feet. One detail that Mila noticed, was that Yulia had a last name that was uncommon in that area. It was the same last name as Pastor Sasha, Young Life Director, who gave us the room in Young Life headquarters to start the Center. When she told him about Yulia and the name of the village, she was from, Sasha was amazed. It was the same village his father was from. He called his mother and asked if there were any relatives left in the village. Her answer was, "Oh, yes! Your father, that left me with you and your brother, when you were 6 years old, had a brother and I believe that his wife and kids are still there." Yes, Yulia was his cousin, he never met! And now she needed help. One day when Yulia came to the Life Center for the motherhood classes, Sasha was waiting for her in the room. They sat down across the table and Sasha said to her, "Yulia, hi! I am your cousin, and my name is Sasha. I have a wife and 6 children, and I'll be so glad to have you stay with us until you are able to support yourself and your children." What a shock for an 18 years old pregnant girl in a new city, far from home and all she knew before coming here. Soon Yulia gave birth to a beautiful baby boy and named him Timothy. She moved to her newly found cousin's house and after a few months it was Sasha who prayed in church over his great nephew Timothy, saved from abortion. God used so many people and the chain of events to form a safety net for the little boy who was on the road to death but was saved by His grace. What could be seen as a chain of coincidences, was very clearly God's plan for Timothy and his mom. Now Yulia is married with three children; she is a wonderful, caring woman. Over the years she had become a great friend of Life Center. This is a story of grace, the story of Timothy. And now he is a happy boy marching to school to start his first grade! It was an amazing moment caught on camera and ended up on the cover of our first Annual Impact Report.

Chapter 7

GOD'S PLAN IN MOTION

THERE IS ALWAYS the first time we try something, when everything is a blur. There is no guarantee that it will work. The first venture becomes a model, good or bad, and the next venture you base on the first one. You either want to replicate it or never repeat it again. In my case, our first Life Center was the model that we knew we had to improve. It was like a first-born baby, everything else was based on what we learned from the first. The word was spreading in the city about our Life Center and a few weeks later, the second pregnant girl had become our client. The local doctor told us that the young girl pregnant with twins was admitted to the hospital after a beating by her husband and was at risk of going into premature labor. Her name was Nadia, and she had no place to live as her husband kicked her out of their apartment in the middle of the night. Mila and Dina decided to visit Nadia and brought her some food in the hospital. In the beginning, she wasn't very receptive. Being an orphan, she didn't use to trust strangers, especially "weird ones" that brought her food, smiled, offered help and didn't ask anything in return. But slowly, Nadia's heart started to open up. Especially, when she gave birth to a beautiful girl and boy, and our girls had become the only ones she could trust and rely on. When Nadia got out of the hospital, our center volunteers had become her closest friends and helpers. With the help of the church, they had found her a place to live with the kids (she had an older 7-year-old son) and covered the rent cost for a while. Oksana had become part of the "Life Center Family", as she started to call us and started to attend the church.

Nadia with her twins, 2017

One Sunday, I received a text message that said, "Nadia gave her heart to Jesus today!" with a picture of her standing in front of the church with Pastor Slavik next to her, praying to God and blessing Nadia and her kids. What an amazing turn of events! One year later I had the privilege to witness Nadia's baptism and her three kids were with her. Those are the moments in life when I realize how God in His sovereign plan works through us! He gave me such a privilege to be a witness to the miracle of transformation from sinner to Child of God! Nadia had become a new person in Him! A couple years later she married a friend who became a solider, and now she is the wife of a solider who is defending his country in this terrible war with Russia. Nadia's life is not easy. But God's grace is with her and her beautiful children! It is such a joy to see how they have grown in front of our eyes. I still see them occasionally when I visit Ukraine. God's plan was in motion!

Six months after the opening of our Chernivtsy Life Center, we were invited by Pastor Alex to the city of Lutsk to open what is now our second Life Center in their city. That is how the idea of the whole network of Life Centers came to life.

Then was the Life Center in Zaporizhia.

I still am amazed by the joy and positive spirit of our Zaporizhia's team. Under the guidance of wonderful woman Elina, who trusted God even after the losses of her children, to have courage and tremendous love for the pregnant women in crisis. Today Zaporizhia Life Center is under constant missile attacks, and they are very close to the front line. Despite all this they are growing tremendously and faithfully serving women refugees in the most difficult circumstances.

After the second Life Center, there was the third and on and on it goes. I received a phone call from a woman named Lena, who moved to Poland with her family many years ago. Before that, she started postabortion ministry in her hometown Poltava by giving her testimony in the local church. She didn't even realize how many women related to her. So many souls, broken by abortion, were coming forward and reaching out for help. Soon she and a few other women started to counsel abortion minded women saving lives in the city of Poltava.

Not long after the move to Poland, Lena started to attend a Ukrainian speaking church in Gdansk. And again, she shared her testimony about abortion and the amazing healing she found in Christ. People in the church encouraged her to start ministering and that is when she reached out to me with the invitation to open a Life Center in Gdansk.

"Another country, God?" I wasn't ready! I didn't speak the language! But God was clear in His calling, and I went to Poland. It took us two years to form and train the team and prepare everything needed for the opening of our first Polish Life Center.

In 2019 "Save a Life International Foundation Polska" came into existence. We were prepared to serve Polish women, but there were some Ukrainians that were part of the team. We didn't understand fully then, but God knew in advance. He knew that three years later, millions of women, pregnant and with little children would be flooding the Polish cities and villages seeking shelter from the war that Russia started at the beginning of 2022. Our Life Center had a new purpose. We had to rent another building to host 15 pregnant women. Our Ukrainian volunteers were overwhelmed with work, but they were tireless. "This is the time to serve and save lives," they were telling me.

Again, we didn't know what the future held, but God knew, and we obeyed. What a joy to see that following His calling bears such fruit.

LERA'S STORY

One of my favorite experiences when I visit Ukraine is attending the summer camps for our moms. Usually when someone says "camp" they mean summer camps for children or youth. It has to be somewhere in the mountains or by the sea and the program and activities should be fun. When we first heard "Young mom's camp" from our friends Ira and Sasha from Young Life, we loved the idea! Not all our moms were young, but they needed time to relax too. Imagine the women who had just gone through a terrible crisis, often left alone with the baby and sometimes with more older children. These women couldn't afford a luxury such as a vacation. They could hardly support themselves and their babies. Many of them had never been on a real vacation! This is why this idea of the weeklong camps for moms had become so popular, and after a couple of camps, it became an important part of our organizational programs. It became an amazing time of reflection, games, and fun, deep midnight conversations. The camps had become a place where women lowered their guards. They could become little girls again with dreams, hopes, and conversations. They didn't have to pretend or perform. Our designated volunteers took care of their children while mothers were fully served and pampered.

One summer I visited our mom's camp in Zaporizhzhia. Our local Life Center team rented the old Soviet Era youth campground resort. Some dormitories were abandoned but the one we rented overlooked the beautiful riverbank of Dnipro River. The colorful wildflowers made the place look so welcoming and cheerful. The moms had a blast playing games outside, walking in small groups with the strollers or with their babies in their arms, laughing, and telling stories about their lives. When I approached them and was introduced, they were a little confused and didn't know how to behave, but after a few words and hugs, everyone relaxed and went back to the way there were before. The women were eager to tell me who they were, express how grateful they were for such an opportunity to be here, and wanted to know more about me. After all, I am an American, looking and speaking like a Ukrainian. Then I noticed one young girl, with a beautiful baby girl in a stroller, kind of staying behind the crowd and not saying a word. I went to her and asked her name. "My name is Lera," she answered shyly. "I am Yana's sister." "Our volunteer Yana?" I tried to clarify.

"Yes, my sister Yana has been serving on the Life Center team since it opened. I remembered how Yana had asked me and all our team to pray for Lera, her younger sister, who was going to go through with an abortion and didn't want to listen to any arguments against it. Lera told Yana that she was pregnant, her boyfriend didn't want the baby, and he wasn't even around anymore. So, no matter what, Lera was determined to abort the baby. After telling Yana about her pregnancy, Lera disappeared, and all Yana could do was to pray for her. That is when she asked the team to join her in the fight for Lera and her baby. Time passed by and Lera called again, and after a long conversation, agreed to come to the center for a consultation. That is how her journey to God began. The girls at the Life Center surrounded Lera with love and care for her unborn baby without any reservations. Lera started attending the classes for future moms and eventually started to go to the church with her sister. After Lera gave birth to a beautiful baby girl, her boyfriend Sasha came back and asked if he could see the baby. He showed remorse for his cowardly behavior and drinking habits. He started to assume responsibility for Lera and his daughter. One day they both were invited to the Christian Couples Retreat organized by the church, and some of our volunteers from the center brought them there. Sasha was so amazed by the men he met there. He never had a good example of the father or a husband. Since he was little, he was surrounded by drinking men and thought that this is how life is. To his surprise, he saw a completely different picture! He met wonderful loving couples that loved each other and God. That retreat had become Sasha's turning point in life. He gave his life to Christ and promised to live by a different standard.

Soon after the retreat, Lera and Sasha got married in the church and our Life Center team gave them a small, beautiful reception. Now Lera and Sasha have two beautiful girls and Lera is volunteering alongside her sister and helping other girls who are in the place she used to be. She is helping them to make the choice for life. These are the precious encounters with our women that make me want to go forward when life gets tough, when circumstances are not in my favor, and when resources are low.

THE NOTES ON THE BATHROOM MIRROR.

It is not a secret that no matter how big your ministry is, how fast it grows and how successful it is, the feelings of uncertainty, inadequacy, fear, and exhaustion overpower the leader behind the closed doors. Especially, when the work is done, the speeches finished, and the questions answered. Sometimes when I am brushing my teeth in front of my bathroom mirror it hits me. What do I see? The girl that hides her insecurities behind the big smile, the woman who suffered grief and disappointments, or the leader who has people following her and is so scared to disappoint them. What do I see in the mirror? I see a face that is no longer young but not old either. Small wrinkles have started to settle here and there. I see that some things that I was hoping to still have time for, will never come to be, but it's ok. Some dreams that I still hope for might never come true, and it's okay too. God only knows, and it doesn't give me the right to look into the future without hope. I have in front of me on my bathroom mirror two little notes; one was given to me casually by my old friend and another I wrote myself. Both notes were put on my bathroom mirror years ago, when I was starting Save a Life International. I stuck them in the mirror's wooden frame as a reminder and encouragement to continue my journey. The first note I have written for myself as God's reassurance says:

> "The Lord will keep you from all harm- he will watch over your coming and going both now and forevermore." Psalm 121:7

The second note is a prophetic one. We were at breakfast with my friend Felisia, and suddenly she pulled this flash card from her jeans' back pocket and gave it to me. "Here, take it," she said. It was out of blue. She didn't write it for me. She probably wrote it for herself, but God knew I had to have it. And I got it. He was telling me something then, and He is still whispering to me every time I look in the mirror. Here is what it says:

> "I will go before you and will level the mountains; I will break down the gates of bronze and cut through bars of iron. I will give you hidden treasures, riches stored in secret places, so that you may know that I am the Lord, the God of Israel, who summons you by name." Isaiah 45:2

"Amen! Amen! Jesus, I love You."

That note was given to me when I had no funds whatsoever to start my ministry. I was looking at this note and didn't really understand and believe that it could actually happen to me. But it was written in the Bible, and the note was given to me! Every day I would look at it and ask God, "Really God? What does this note have to do with me? And He slowly started to show me, miracle after miracle, His generosity never left me for a moment. I just had to be careful to recognize it when it came and give Him the Glory! Now when I brush my teeth, I look in the mirror, and I see the two notes that have been there for the last 8 years. None of them disappointed me, because it was the word of God, my Daddy, who calls me by my name. He is watching over me, over my past and future, over my dreams and hopes and over my disappointments.

He knows, He provides, He is enough......

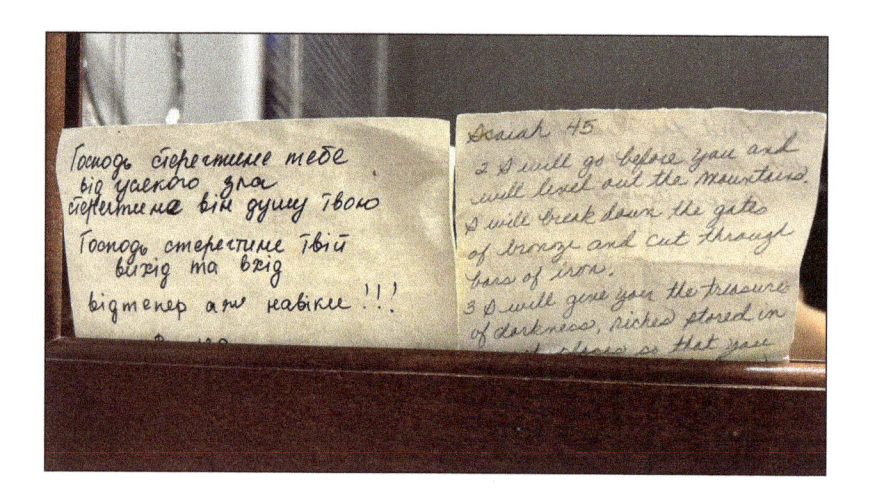

Notes on the mirror

Sometimes I look back on the last 8 years of Save a Life and its 12 Life Centers, where over one thousand babies have been saved from abortion and so many women have gone through the amazing transformation, and I am amazed. Over 150 volunteers give their time, money, and skills every day to make a difference in the women's lives.

Our Life Centers are in 3 Countries and the plan is to have Life Centers in every major city of Ukraine, Poland, and wherever else God sends us to serve and love women without judgement.

None of this would have happened without an amazing leadership team. Starting with the very first leaders that I described earlier and all who have come after. Their names are

GOD'S PLAN IN MOTION

Alla, Elina, Iryna, Elena, Natalka, Kristina, Natalya, Oksana, Paulina, Victoria, Toma, and Olga and I know more are yet to come. Each of these women have their own unique stories of suffering, loss, brokenness, and grief. Also, each one has joy, enthusiasm, courage, love, persistence, and many more amazing qualities that make them leaders that others want to follow. Each of these women deserve at least a chapter in this book, but I hope that those chapters will be put together for a separate book, called "Sali History" that one day will become a wonderful testimony of God's grace and inspiration. There is the saying going around about Save a Life that anyone who comes to work for us either gets married or if already married, gets pregnant. This saying is not based on hearsay, it has been proven many times.

What people consider the weakness, God turns into the strength and beauty. Natalia is a very great example of this.

One day while in Ukraine, Mila, then director of Chernivtsi Life Center received a phone call. The girl's name was Natalia and she sounded very straight forward. "I heard about the work you do with the women, and I would like to have a ministry like this in our city. I am a nurse and would like to help women in crisis, because I have had many encounters with pregnant women who came to get an abortion in our hospital and realized that they have no place to receive any information about an alternative to abortion." She was so persistent and positive that is seemed almost too pushy! To tell you the truth, I didn't take this phone call seriously. When Mila asked me what we should do, I said, "That girl is funny," and reluctantly agreed to meet with Natalia. I told her she could come to our Life Center in

Chernivtsy, check it out for herself, and after she could decide if she was still interested in such a ministry. To my surprise, she asked if she could come the next day. Really?! It was the end of my trip and in two days I was going back home to the US, but I decided to give it a chance.

The next morning there was a knock on the door and Natalia walked in with a big smile on her face! Never mind that she took three buses and was on the road for at least 6 hours. Also, when we asked where she would be staying overnight, she casually said, "I will go back home tonight after speaking with you." Wow! That's the spirit!

We spent a couple of hours getting to know each other and telling Natalia about Save a Life's mission and vision and what we were looking for in the person that would be leading the future Life Center team of volunteers. We gave her the list of all the steps to start the new center from finding the right passionate people, going through the training, and the final steps to have a grand opening. Natalia listened carefully and asked a lot of questions. After most of the things were explained, she thanked us and said that she would be contacting us in a few months.

It is embarrassing for me to admit that I am guilty of judging people by their looks. That was exactly how I reacted. Natalia was dressed very simple, even too simple. To be honest, I would never have thought of her as a leader, until God proved me, wrong the hard way. Natalia never thought of herself as a leader either. She gathered a team of women and men and started to talk with them about the idea of opening a Life Center in their city. A few months later Mila, Dina, and I were training the new team and were working on opening the center in the city of Khmelnitsky. All this time, Natalia was doing everything that needed to be done, only no one even considered her as a future director. In my view, the person representing our organization should be the bright, outgoing, and good-looking girl. Eventually, we picked one promising lady from the team and trained her to lead the team. After few more months of training the Life Center in Khmelnitsky was opened.

What a disappointment it was for me to find out only after a few days that it was a total disaster. I cannot tell all the details, but we had to look for another leader as fast as we could and God forgive me, I was following the same pattern; outgoing and good-looking girl, only to be proven that I am wrong again. The team didn't perform, volunteers were not united, and the center didn't grow and develop as fast as other centers did during the same period of time. Six months later, we were right where we started. Lord, what is wrong? What are we missing? And He clearly showed me that I didn't ask Him to show me who should lead the Life Center. I was using my own experience and judgment. After dismissing the whole team, we decided to ask Natalia to take charge. After all, she was the one who came to us at the first, who cared most about Save a Life's mission, and who humbly stayed in the shadows, doing all the hard work, unnoticed. We finally noticed her and trusted God with His choice. And we watched how He did His powerful work through this humble but faithful girl.

Natalia was 34 and single. When she was little girl, she was diagnosed with a physical condition and was expected to be handicapped for the rest of her life. Thanks to the persistence of her father, she learned to walk with a little limp, graduated nursing school, and got a job at the local hospital. She herself admits that because of her condition she was often overlooked and neglected. She didn't believe much of herself, but she believed that Jesus knows her and believes in her. That was enough for her to have a positive spirit about everything she did. When Natalia became the director, amazing things started to happen. Many new women started to call and ask for help, new great volunteers joined the team, and the old ones returned with the different attitude. Suddenly, God started to show His miracles and many new babies were saved from abortion in that city. Even more, Natalia met a wonderful man and got married. The doctors told her that with her condition she will not be able to have kids, but God gave them two beautiful girls and now Natalia and her husband are both SALI staff. The Center in Khmelnitsky has become one of the most successful Centers in Ukraine.

I am grateful to God for teaching me this lesson! He was gently and patiently waiting until I recognized my helplessness and when I did, he started to work.

> "So He said to me, "This is the word of the Lord to Zerubbabel: 'Not by might nor by power, but by my Spirit, says the Lord Almighty.'" Zechariah 4:6

I wish I could mention every wonderful leader that joined our team over the years.

Each of them came to Save a Life because of their passion for women and their unborn babies. They all were ready to serve without pay, giving their time and talents to the ministry. They formed the teams, reached out to the community, and underwent training to counsel women in crisis. But the one quality that all our leaders possess it is ability to love. To love the women who might not appreciate or even notice it. To love not just with words, but with their deeds. That is who our leaders are. They are the people who drive the Save a Life International by God's Power working in them.

I heard the expression from my friend "life is like a train, when it is in full speed it is not that simple to slow it down or stop it". That is how Save a Life had become. God started it and brought it to full speed and no one, not even me could stop it. Not even the Global Pandemic that came so suddenly that no one was prepared to face it could stop what God was doing.

Chapter 8

WHEN EVERYTHING SHUTS DOWN, WE OPEN UP

LOOKING BACK AT the Covid pandemic times, it is hard to believe that the whole world could be shut off in a matter of days. A lot of people were skeptical, and many remain skeptical even now. Those who lost their loved ones experienced the reality of what could happen. The times were so crazy.

Our annual leaders retreat was scheduled for the beginning of March 2020, and we all got together in Kyiv excited to spend the next 3 days planning our work, training, and developing new strategies to serve our clients. To tell you the truth, we already heard about this pandemic, but it was far somewhere in China. The first cases were starting to show in Europe and the U.S., but nobody expected such a turn of events. The first two days of our retreat were good. On the third day, the news started to come in that some countries started to close their borders, and flights were canceled. My husband called me and said, "Nadia, you better fly home as soon as you can book a flight. In a few days America will be closing the borders." I remember we were having dinner with our leaders in the local restaurant, and I was trying frantically to change my ticket to a closer day, but all I saw in my United app was "cancelled". Calling airlines was not an option, because all lines were busy. Finally, I realized that I could be stuck away from my home and family indefinitely. Fortunately, I was able to find a new ticket home and later found out it was the last plane from Ukraine to the US before the long and exhausting year of the pandemic. Yes, I got home right in time. When I arrived, my staff called me from Ukraine and said that the country was in lock down. All our leaders had to figure out how to get home to their cities, because in one day, all public transportation was stopped. Train routes were stopped. They were on their own, as was the rest of the people in the country.

That's when Zoom, Google Meet, and other online communication became essential for so many organizations. The world was changing right before our eyes and there was not much we could do. Or so we thought, at first. But then creativity started to do its work, and we started to adjust and figure out ways to serve out women. Mila, our Ukrainian director told me, "It's time for us to be creative as never before. Let's get the protective wardrobe and start distributing all the necessary supplies to our moms with children, who are stranded in the house." Slowly, we started to develop the strategy on how to serve our clients through the communication online. Whole courses were adjusted to online format and believe it or not, we started to expend and have more women calling for help or advise or consultation. Many people were so depressed or scared that the cheerful tone of voice and uplifting demeanor of our counselors were like a breath of fresh air for single moms with a baby on the way or those caring for a newborn.

Isn't it amazing how fear can dictate the way we live and interact?

I'll never forget how people were easily angered at each other over something as simple as a mask. Some were for it; some were against it. Nobody knew for sure what was going on. Then vaccinations became available. It spurred another controversy. The world turned into a fearful angry place. It is unbelievable how fear can turn friends into enemies. For some, it was the time when everything stopped, but for Save a Life it became a time of many opportunities to serve people and show them the love of Christ. Those who know God are free from the fear of death and the pandemic gave us the chance to reach out to places where others couldn't or wouldn't reach.

Chapter 9

THE WAR...
RUSSIAN INVASION OF UKRAINE

FEBRUARY 24, 2023... The memory is vague. I remember my newly renovated kitchen, and my husband sitting at the island. He said, "Nadia, Russians are bombing Ukraine...This is the war..." Our eyes were glued to the screens of our Ipads, reading the news. It was all surreal...

My first thought was that I needed to call my girls in Ukraine. I called a Zoom meeting. The faces of my leaders started to pop up on the screen. One, after another, after another. Their usually happy faces were full of disbelief. It couldn't be happening. We were attacked.

The first thing that came to my mind was to let them know that they and their families were my priority. If they had to evacuate, get to safety, they should. Elina was 38 weeks pregnant and her city Zhaporizhzhia was attacked by missiles. Victoria, our Life Center Director from the US was in Kyiv at that time going through IVF to have her baby. Natalia from Khmelnitsky just had her baby girl a couple months prior. Svetlana from

Pokrovsk had a four-month-old baby boy. They were all mothers and our Life Center Directors.

Iryna from Odessa, Alla and Kristina from Chernivtsy, and Elenka from Poltava were also on the call. We all prayed together and discussed situations. They all chose to stay where they were, develop a plan to evacuate our moms if needed, and to see how we could take care of the most vulnerable. One day at a time…That's all we could figure out.

It was 4 pm and my husband and I were still in the kitchen. We realized that we haven't had breakfast or lunch. I was in my morning robe, making phone calls to our politicians asking them to intervene. I remember one of them calling me back, assuring that he would do everything possible to appeal to the American congress on behalf of Ukraine. We were creating the petition, figuring out how to write it, and deciding how to ask people to sign it. In our petition, we asked the American government to give Ukraine weapons, to close the sky, and to protect Ukraine by following the Budapest Memorandum agreement. We had to do something! We had to try!

The next day we went to Washington DC to ask for support of Ukraine. We marched with the hundreds of our fellow Ukrainians in front of the Capitol. And then, day after day, we saw in the news the bombings and the destruction of our homeland. The worst part was that we were far away!

Then the thought came to my mind, "I must be there with my girls, my Save a Life family. My life in no way had more value than theirs. I looked at my husband and my son and they knew I had to go.

On March 1st I was on a plane flying to Poland and then to Romania to get to the Ukrainian border, where my Operation Director Alla was working with the refugees, transporting them in our van through the border into safety.

I remember when in Warsaw I saw our Polish staff Marlena and Elena at the airport. The tears started to flow down my cheeks. We embraced, we cried, and we realized that this time everything was different. Our Poland Life Center was turned into a refugee camp. The church we worked with was full of Ukrainian people. My heart was aching for the little children playing on the mattresses in the church hallways, not realizing that their homes were destroyed, and their future was stolen by war. The young mothers with the babies were trying to adjust in the common rooms that would be their home for a while until they were transported to other places further and further away from the lives they were forced to leave behind.

After a couple days in Poland, I headed to Romania to the town that bordered with Ukraine. When I landed in Iasi airport, I was shocked. It was so crowded! Women, men, and children were sitting on the floors and standing in lines to get through security to get on the next plane to Europe. It was again so surreal like I was in a war movie. Only I wasn't in a movie, it was a war. The war started and its effects had spilled over Europe. Over 7 million Ukrainians had fled the country in a matter of months.

Alla and I, 2022

Alla met me at the entrance, and we drove away toward the Ukrainian border. She brought me to a beautiful campground in the mountains, which was converted to a refugee camp thanks to the generosity of the owner Cornel Clipa. Cornel and his wife Owana opened their place to the refugees from the first days of war. They would pick them up at the border crossing, bring them to the camp, feed them, and let them rest for a couple days. That's how Alla met them when she transported women out through the border and Cornel offered them the place to stay and rest. Then Alla had to go back and bring more women and children and this time she took them strait to Cornel's camp. Again, and again and again. That is where she brought me that night. The first morning I came into the dining room and offered help. They pointed that the floor needed cleaning, and I got to work. Then Alla came in and said that we had to go to the border to pick up more people. And we went. Back and forth, back and forth. I will never forget the faces of the men and women, so lost, still not comprehending the scale of this tragedy.

THE WHOLE LIFE IN ONE BAG.

One night we received a call from our volunteer Luba, asking us to meet her friend with his family at the border where we were helping and take them to our camp, until they could continue their journey to Germany. The man's name was Sergey. He was in his late 60s and was with his wife and their baby, his 80 years old mother, sister, his daughter with two children and another female in law. When we picked them up, they were so exhausted from being on the road for two weeks, that they couldn't talk much. We fed them that night, and they went to bed. The next morning at the breakfast they shared their story.

Sergey lived in Kharkiv, a beautiful city on the border with Russia. By the time he turned 60 he had a successful shoe factory business, beautiful house, and growing family. I complimented them on the baby, thinking the little girl was theirs, although his wife was close to his age. Sergey responded with a sad smile, "This is our granddaughter Liya. Her mom, our daughter -in -law, died from Covid right after her birth. My son went on a business trip to Germany the week before the war started and Liya was with us.

The first two weeks of the bombings we stayed in the basement, but when the food became scarce and our old mother got sicker, we started to look for ways to get out of the city. That's when the rocket hit our house, destroying the car and everything around, and our factory was completely destroyed. We had to evacuate as soon as possible to save ourselves."

It took two weeks for them to get to the Romanian border, where we picked them up. Sergey showed me the pictures of his house after the bombings, and said with tears in his eyes, "All my life I worked hard, thinking that I would enjoy my retirement with my kids and grandkids next to me. But now that is what I have left," and he pointed his finger to the big plastic bag and the small suitcase. "All my life is in this plastic bag."

I will never forget those words, the Lord reminder how unpredictable our life can be.

FAST FORWARD TO SEPTEMBER 19, 2023.

Today, Alla arrived from Ukraine to participate in our Annual Fundraising Banquet here in Philadelphia, PA. Every year since my Save a Life Journey started, we organize Fundraising Dinners to where local people from different churches and organizations in our area love to come, eat Ukrainian food, and support our efforts. Even during the Covid year we still had our Picnic/Fundraiser at my church. Through the years, we developed close relationships with many supporters and some of them attend every year. Those are my favorite sweet older ladies Sofia and Nina. I can't imagine our banquet without them. I know that their prayers keep us going. They don't have a lot of money, but their prayers carried me through the years of many ups and downs. Those are the faithful ones.

Alla is one of the faithful ones too. Young widow with two children, she came to Save a Life right after her husband died from cancer. In the beginning she came as a volunteer, then she was a Life Center Director, and now she runs all SALI operations in Ukraine. She was the one who initiated the evacuation of our women with children when the war started. She was the one I joined at the Romanian border. She is a fearless, focused, and strong woman who goes in the midst of conflict and solves the problem as if nothing big were happening. No one could tell that after all was done, this strong girl that everyone was asking for help, hoping that she knew the answer, would be quietly crying into her pillow, mourning the love of her life. No one could tell that behind this facade of strength there was a sweet young woman, weak and tender. That is my Alla. My co-worker and my friend. It was wonderful to have her with me in America for a short visit. We drank tea and I showed her a little book made from the "Facebook memories" of the year 2022, the year when the war started, and I decided to order a hard copy as a reminder of this life changing time. We both looked at the pictures and saw our faces, with no make-up, dark circles under our eyes showing the lack of sleep. We saw the faces of refugees we helped and volunteers that worked with us. Some may think these are not the memories to make into a book, but for us, we wanted to remember.

BLANKETS OVER THE FENCE

While I was helping with relief efforts, there was a humanitarian convoy with food supplies, warm clothes, and blankets going into Ukraine. I was in one of the vans bringing supplies to our centers. There was a long crossing pathway at the border between Ukraine and Romania, that had wire fence on both sides leading to the check point. I saw hundreds of women, children, and elderlies with bags standing in line in the freezing weather.

I heard children crying and saw elderly ladies behind the wire fence trembling from the cold. Mothers were holding their babies, crying themselves from fear and desperation. I didn't know what to do, or how to help. Suddenly, I realized that we had a lot of blankets in the back of our van! I asked the driver to stop, jumped out of the van, and asked him to open the back of the van and help me. I literally dove into the piles on supplies and started to pull the blankets out one by one! It was a funny, ridiculous picture, but I got blankets and started to throw them over the fence. People were catching them and wrapping themselves and their children. Soon other drivers stopped and started to help me. It was an interesting scene. Officers at the border didn't know how to react at first, but then they just ignored us and let us finish what we started. This "blanket" situation seemed of so little help, but at that moment it was all we could do. I remember the grateful eyes of the mother who wrapped her child in the blanket and an old lady thanking us through the wired fence. It was such a small gesture, but it was from our hearts.

After we unloaded all the supplies, we had to cross the border into Romania before the martial law time. It was around 10 pm when we approached the customs check point, and I saw a scene that has stuck with me to this day. I remember looking at the crowd of refugees and I realized that with this volume of people they would be stranded there for the whole night until the next morning. One of our drivers suddenly turned to me and said, "Let's try to load our vans with as many women and children as we can. Let's try to get them through the border."

Border crossing, 2022

We stopped and got out of our vans. The whole convoy stopped, and we started shouting in the crowd that we can take as many women with little children as would fit in our vehicles. Women started to run toward us. All our drivers were helping them into the vans. The van I was in had 3 front seats and the empty space in the back where all the cargo had been unloaded in Ukraine. There was the driver Albert, and I was in the passenger seat. When I got out from the van, my eyes spotted one woman with a toddler and her elderly parents. How can we separate them? What should we do?

"Hey, Nadia," Albert said, "Can you drive stick shift?" Hmmm…. I drove stick shift when I lived in Ukraine 26 years ago. "Sure," I answered without thinking. I didn't understand at first, but then he explained. "If you get behind the wheel there will be more room for the refugees. Without thinking for too long, I invited the woman with her baby and her mother to our van, the grandpa had to go to another van, and Albert, our driver started to walk next to the vehicle through the check points. It took us an hour and a half to cross the check points into Romania and the family that was in our van were spared from waiting in the freezing weather all night. That night, our convoy transported over 70 people through the border to safety. We got to our base long after midnight, tired and dirty but very happy, knowing that 70 more people were taken into the safety.

Those are the memories from the first month of this horrible war. As I write this book, the war is still going on and has been for almost two years. When my husband and I sat in our kitchen looking at our Ipads in March 2022, we couldn't even imagine that it was only the beginning. We didn't think that in the following months horrific events would take place in Ukrainian cities, and that thousands of civilians would be killed, and women and children tortured and raped. I didn't know that there would be much worse conditions ahead of our people. And maybe it is a blessing that we can't know our future. It gave us the ability to fight, hope, and move ahead with the hope that the future would be better.

Chapter 10

LIFE AND WORK DURING THE WAR

AFTER A FEW months of heavy bombings and territories captures by Russian soldiers where they plundered the land, destroyed the houses, and raped and killed hundreds of women and children, we realized that our mission was even more vital than ever. All our Life Centers were hosting refugees, giving out food packages, and comforting the suffering people. Then slowly we realized that many humanitarian missions, churches, or just regular folks were doing the same things. Our focus returned to the pregnant women. You can feed the person, give her shelter and clothes, but you can't relieve the wrenching fear in the stomach. The food can't take away the despair and hopelessness that clouds the judgment of the woman whose husband was killed in the war, whose house burned down, and who has no future. Those women had no other choice, than to go to the hospital and ask for an abortion. Pain, fear, anger, and depression are always the factors in crisis pregnancy. But the war brought many more struggles including war trauma which became an everyday topic.

> **You can feed the person, give her shelter and clothes, but you can't relieve the wrenching fear in the stomach.**

Our staff had their own struggles, the war didn't leave anyone untouched. To be able to help other women while your own house is destroyed, and your husband or brother is on the front lines facing death every day is inspiring. My team would get up in the morning, thinking of the new girls, that needed help and the load of other issues to deal with and serve with compassion. These are our Sali leaders, our counselors, our staff, and volunteers.

I remember Elina telling me, with tears in her eyes, the news about a young family who died from the Russian missile that destroyed a whole apartment building a few blocks from our Life Center. The young woman Kamila came to our Life Center when she was pregnant and in crisis. She decided to keep the baby in spite of a difficult situation in her personal life and attended our programs all through the pregnancy. Then she moved to another city with her husband and the father of the soon to be born baby. And then the war came. This is what we saw in the local paper:

"Today, March 9, little Emilia Furnyk was supposed to be 8 months old, but the child did not live to this day. She was killed along with her parents–Kamila and Ilya–by a Russian missile on March 2. The bodies of the family were found under the rubble two days later. They were all in the same bed.

Kamila and Ilya met in Zaporizhzhia, studied together at an aviation college, and then worked at Motor Sich," says Kamila's aunt Tetyana. The war caught up with them in the region where they were visiting. The pregnant woman hid from the shelling in the basement. Then they managed to leave, they were in the west of Ukraine where the baby Emilia was born. Later they returned home. We lived in Ilya's father's apartment. They were supposed to redecorate it, but they never got a chance, says Kamila's aunt."

The life of baby Emilia was spared from abortion, but less than a year later was taken by the war… How can this be fair? These are the questions we had to ask every day. They are questions that we can't have answers to. We are fighting for life every day, while evil people contemplate destroying this very life, all because someone with the power decides that he has the right to kill. It makes me think, what is the difference between killing children who are outside of the mother's womb with weapons and killing the same children who are still inside of their mother's womb with a scalpel or a pill. What is the difference? People can find millions of arguments, but life is always sacred. It is growing, moving, and has the right to develop. The most fundamental right to life, is given by our Creator.

Chapter 11

LIFE OR DEATH

WHAT IS THE best way to understand the woman in crisis? We are talking about The Woman, the beautiful creation that was granted an amazing gift to give life to another human being. To carry LIFE inside of her body and feel it growing and moving, kicking, and reacting to the noises from outside. People often ask me if I am pro-life or pro-choice, like it has an opposite meaning. How fast and easy we put a label on people without even thinking. I am for LIFE, and I am for Choice. It is up to me to decide which one to choose LIFE or DEATH. They are both choices, aren't they?

When I first came to Ukraine on the invitation of my friend Olga, I saw those words already picked by her "Save a Life". It was clear as a daylight that this is the mission God picked for me. One night after I shared my journey and the story of my baby's premature birth and the loss of him with the group of people, one lady came to me and said with the tears in her eyes: "Your little son Jonathan had accomplished his mission so you could carry on and continue to save the babies like him from the violent death by abortion."

Later, after meeting with the women in crisis I wanted to add that not only babies, but women need saving too! The girls who have never been loved the right way, abused, or threatened, humiliated, maybe laughed at. Maybe it is the wife who was told by someone how to live her life and had no voice to speak for herself, because no one will listen. Maybe it's just a respectable woman who just made a mistake, and so scared to live with the consequences. They are all different and each has her own story to tell. Each one is scared and often alone with her crisis and fears.

They all need to hear that someone cares.

"No woman should feel the need to abort her child simply because no one was there to offer her support."

My life continues to unravel, and the New Horizons are still ahead of me, ahead of my beloved SALI family. I don't know the future, but I know God's grace. That is why we obediently following His voice, following these three:

"SANCTITY OF LIFE, WOMEN'S DIGNITY AND LOVE."

I want to end with the beautiful lyrics of the song I recorded many years ago.

I hope the words will touch your heart as it touched and inspired me.

LIFE OR DEATH

When things seem uncertain, when I cannot see
What may come tomorrow to try and test me
My path may be uncharted, still I know by grace
That His mercy endureth and there will be sufficient grace

I don't know the future, but I do know His Grace
And some things I'm unsure of, but in all things I praise
The One who will keep me, till we meet face to face
I don't know the future, but I do know His grace

When my life is over and my work is done
I'll turn to look behind me to see from where I have come
Then I'll know I fought the good fight and I finished my race
But for no other reason, except by His Grace

TO JESUS BE ALL THE GLORY!

For the speaking arrangements, please contact Nadia Gordynsky at **ngordynsky@gmail.com**

You can find out more about Save a Life International at **www.savealifeintl.org**

BIO:

NADIA GORDYNSKY IS the Founder, President and CEO of Save a Life International, the organization that helps women in crisis pregnancy, helps the victims of abuse and domestic violence.

Nadia has been a speaker and performer of Christian music for 25 years and is the author of four albums.

Being Native Ukrainian she is actively taking part in the events organized by Ukrainian diaspora in United Nations, New York and Mission to Ukraine at the Ukrainian Embassy in USA. Nadia is a strong advocate for women in crisis situations and promotes the ideas of Sanctity of Life, Women's Dignity and Love.

Nadia is married to her husband Vladimir and they have three children on this Earth, Olesya, Luda and Johnny. Johnathan is waiting for them in Heaven.